JULY 2015

Love me, love my dog!!

When I got Frankie as a gift

for my 40th birthday I was head over

heels in love at first sight!! He is such

a sweet little dog and who could resist that

adorable face!!! If you are going to hang

around with me...you really

MUST love

gettin' air

wilk

nose blunt • feeble • bowls • half cap flip • indy

overcrook • 5-0 • melon • skate

landed it • tre flip • rails • ollie

nosegrind • skate park • tranny • rad

chill • sick • boardslide

SKATE

chris & brian

kick flip

One of the most intimidating aspects of creativity is being faced with the blank page in front of you. But luckily creative ideas don't have to be spirited out of thin air. Think of the colors or patterns you are drawn to in everyday life. What composes your wardrobe? Maybe you strut wild funky patterns with retro flair. Or maybe you're all girl with feminine colors, lace and sheer fabrics. What about home décor? Is the spirit of Mexican design alive on your walls with radiant color? Maybe you find your inspiration in the shabby richness of soft pink and baby blue patterns complemented by distressed white wood. What about jewelry, book and magazine covers, even wrapping paper and greeting cards? Think of what you're drawn to when shopping for these items and discover inspiration in the most common places. It's likely the patterns, textures and colors you are drawn to in everyday life will come alive in your scrapbook art. So what is your signature style? Still not sure? This book will help.

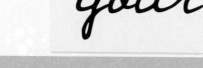

Quick & Easy Scrapbook Styles covers five major scrapbook styles prominently seen in recent publications. These styles are graphic, sassy, urban, fun and funky, and romantic. Each has its own set of unique qualities that distinguishes it from all others. Some pages are feminine, chic and rich in florals and pastels. Others flaunt a jazzy, hip look with vivid colors and psychedelic patterns. Others are clean and crisp, each featuring an impactful photograph as the focal point.

As you browse the pages of this book, you may immediately recognize the style that fits you best, or you may be inspired to experiment with one that's completely new to you. This will give you the opportunity to stretch your imagination and exercise your creative muscle. You may discover that the colors, textures or patterns of a style you haven't tried before offer a fresh and invigorating approach. Or you may find that tried-and-true style your work has always leaned toward is now easier than ever with the clever tips and techniques offered in this book. Wherever this exploration leads you, we hope you'll discover the perfect recipe for creating your own scrapbook masterpieces seasoned to your personal taste!

QUICK & EASY SCRAPBOOK STYLES

From the Editors of MEMORY MAKERS BOOKS

MEMORY MAKERS BOOKS
CINCINNATI, OHIO

10 09 08 07 06   5 4 3 2 1

Distributed in Canada by Fraser Direct
100 Armstrong Avenue
Georgetown, ON, Canada L7G 5S4
Tel: (905) 877-4411

Distributed in the U.K. and Europe by David & Charles
Brunel House, Newton Abbot, Devon, TQ12 4PU, England
Tel: (+44) 1626 323200, Fax: (+44) 1626 323319
E-mail: postmaster@davidandcharles.co.uk

Distributed in Australia by Capricorn Link
P.O. Box 704, S. Windsor, NSW 2756 Australia
Tel: (02) 4577-3555

Library of Congress Cataloging-in-Publication Data
Quick & easy scrapbook styles / The editors of Memory Makers Books.
       p. cm.
   Includes index.
ISBN-13: 978-1-892127-98-3 (pbk. : alk. paper)
ISBN-10: 1-892127-98-9 (pbk. : alk. paper)
  1. Photograph albums. 2. Photographs--Conservation and restoration. 3.
Scrapbooks. I. Memory Makers Books.
   TR501.Q52 2006
   745.593--dc22
                              2006025406

EDITOR: Amy Glander
DESIGNER: Brian Roeth
PRODUCTION COORDINATOR: Matt Wagner
PHOTOGRAPHERS: Christine Polomsky and Tim Grondin
STYLIST: Nora Fink

F+W PUBLICATIONS, INC.

CONTRIBUTING ARTISTS:

Jessie Baldwin

Amber Baley

Joanna Bolick

Vicki Boutin

Nicole Cholet

Renee Coffey

Samuel Cole

Holly Corbett

Marie Cox

Amy Farnsworth

Kathy Fesmire

Becky Fleck

Jennifer Gallacher

Amy Goldstein

Kelly Goree

Greta Hammond

Linda Harrison

Barb Hogan

Nic Howard

Diana Hudson

Jill Jackson-Mills

Kim Kesti

Ki Kruk

Sharon Laakkonen

Melodee Langworthy

Kim Moreno

Kelli Noto

Deb Perry

Suzy Plantamura

Heather Preckel

Torrey Scott

Trudy Sigurdson

Jessica Sprague

Kathleen Summers

Shannon Taylor

Lisa VanderVeen

Courtney Walsh

Susan Weinroth

Angelia Wigginton

table of contents

What's Your Style? • 6

Styles Overview • 7-11

CHAPTER ONE • 12 **graphic**

CHAPTER TWO • 36 **sassy**

CHAPTER THREE • 58 **URBAN**

CHAPTER FOUR • 68 **FUN + FUNKY**

CHAPTER FIVE • 88 *romantic*

Source Guide • 124

Additional Credits & Supplies • 126

Index • 127

graphic

If you love the look of scrapbook pages with clean lines, simple and crisp imagery, bold fonts and lots of open space, then graphic is the style for you. Influenced by the world of graphic design, these pages are trendy and dynamic and are based on real design principals used by professional artists and designers. If this style intrigues you, it's easy to infuse these principles into your pages.

Graphic layouts are often clean and uncluttered, use large or unique type treatments and feature impactful photography. Some pages are geometric—very linear with one large photo as the focal element. Other graphic pages use typography in a creative way as the primary design element. Still others find inpsiration in print ads, brochures or other media to convey a very clean, sophisticated look.

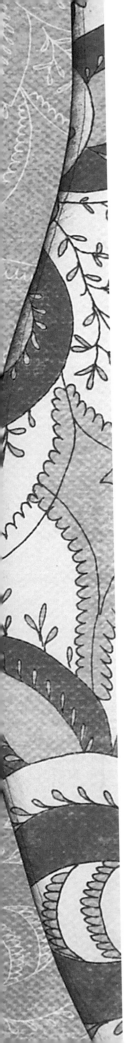

sassy

The sassy style finds its inspiration in fashion. The sassy scrapbooker likes to play "dress up" on her scrapbook page, and she uses items that appeal uniquely to her and then mixes them to create her own personal style.

These pages often use patterns or prints seen in fashion. Flip through the latest copy of *Vogue*, *Cosmo* or *Allure* to get a taste of trends to come. Look to purses, ribbons, fabrics, other accessories and even flowers for inspiration.

The bold approach uses large floral patterns and colors that are bright, vibrant and fun. This variety almost shouts "in your face" with its bold statements.

The bling-bling variation is heavily influenced by jewelry. Often rhinestones, beads, metallics, shimmer and glitter grace these pages. Lots of golds, wild prints and dark colors bring a festive, party feel.

URBAN

The urban style has become increasingly popular in the last few years among crafters who are seeking an extreme, raw, "no boundaries, no rules" approach to scrapbooking. Described as inner-city chic, this style employs a graffiti-like look to make the artwork appear distressed, grungy, dirty and edgy. Images are powerful, gripping and jump off the page. Textures include metal, brick, cement, asphalt, chain link and other unconventional embellishments. Look to publications such as *Rolling Stone*, *Snowboarder* or *The New York Times Upfront* for inspiration on this hip and happening design. Destined to revolutionize scrapbooking, the urban style will transfix you with its citified, world-wise, metropolitan flavor.

FUN + FUNKY

The fun and funky style often boasts free-form abstract shapes and curves. It almost always includes lots of bold and off-beat color choices and designs.

Freestyle and abstract approaches use hand-drawn elements, doodles and free-form shapes such as curves and waves. Textures and prints include lots of unusual color choices and are typically very conceptual.

The retro look uses designs, patterns and color schemes inspired by styles that were prevalent in past decades. The carefree style of retro shapes in bold, unexpected colors results in a fun and funky mood.

Inspiration can also be drawn from pop culture. Look to art, film, music, ads, icons, sayings, slogans and other signs and symbols of the times for ideas for your own pop culture pieces.

romantic

The romantic style is feminine, soft and often tactile and textured. It uses lots of florals and prints, mixing patterns and fabrics.

Trés chic is probably the most well-known romantic style, recognizable by the liberal use of white, florals, pastels, lace and other fibers. Often a distressed white composes the edges or background. Feminine and elegant, the trés chic style uses a variety of altered and layered elements and vintage papers.

The French country style uses polka-dots, crackled wood, red and florals. It can be country folk art or have an international flair. It is warm, welcoming and full of charm.

The Bohemian style is a little bit hippy and a little bit gyspy. Textures are tactile and colors are usually rich and royal. Deep velvets and Asian influences are trademarks of this kind of romantic style.

Glee is the emotion that seems to overcome you, typically in the mid-afternoon when you are well-rested, well-fed, and definitely outside! You exude 100 percent happiness from inside out, and you let it show!

glee

graphic

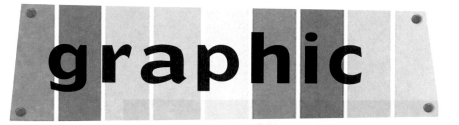

Do you find yourself oohing and aahing over pages that employ crisp lines and clean cuts? If you're drawn to layouts with lots of white space, minimal journaling and strong, impactful photography, the graphic style is for you. These pages can be geometric with strong, linear lines, creatively use type as the primary design element or find their inspiration in print ads, brochures or other media (see page 7 for more details). Keeping the focus on the photos and using modern design principles such as rhythm and unity, the graphic style courses with energy in its lack of embellishment. This style is for any scrapbooker looking to impart a sophisticated look on a fresh, clean page.

DuDe.

You inspire me.

You encourage me.

You keep me positive.

And you'd totally bail me out if I were arrested in Vegas.

love ya.

sassy

As a crafty girl, you know that true style comes by way of using those items that uniquely appeal to you and mixing them to create your own sassy way of expressing yourself. Add a healthy dose of vibrant colors, wild prints, funky beads and starry sequins, and you've got a stunning scrapbook page to call your own. A little bit saucy, a little bit brazen and definitely 100 percent girl, the sassy style finds its inspiration in fashion, jewelry and other items that shimmer and shine (see page 8 for more details). Whether your style leans toward pretty or punk, you'll find a cache of great ideas and examples in this chapter for creating your own sassy scrapbook masterpieces!

my classic girl

Bethany has never been a frilly kind of girl. She loves the tailored look with just a bit of pizazz thrown in. Her "classic" taste carries over to every other part of her life too! Movies, books, cars... you name it... the long-lived titles and styles win her vote every time! Bethany-just my "classic" girl!

SHARON CELEBRATES HER DAUGHTER'S timeless look in this layout by using a traditional black-and-white color palette with just a dash of silver to draw the eye. Finding inspiration in a purse with white leather circles, she decided to adapt the design by using circles to frame the stunning focal photo. A handy circle punch and handwritten journaling kept the page simple and fast. The eyelets, silver flower brads and flower gems add a bit of bling to this sophisticated yet sassy page.

My Classic Girl
Sharon Laakkonen, Superior, Wisconsin

SUPPLIES:

Chipboard letters, flower gems (Heidi Swapp); paper flowers (Prima); flower brads (source unknown); eyelets (Provo Craft); circle punch; pen; cardstock

PRETTY FLOWERS BLOOM on this page featuring Heather's little girl. Heather says she found her inspiration from a purse she saw in an online boutique. She crafted flowers of patterned paper, fabric and buttons to mimic the flowers stitched on the purse and used a white pen to draw faux stitching. Strips of journaling and a handwritten title add whimsy and charm to this sweet page.

Sweet Girl
Heather Preckel, Swannanoa, North Carolina

SUPPLIES:

Patterned paper, stickers (K & Company); fabric (Wal-Mart); fabric brads (Hot Off The Press); brads (Junkitz); foam squares; pen; cardstock; Chestnuts font (Two Peas in a Bucket)

Today was a good day. Hanging with friends. Taking a few pictures. I am content. Feel pretty, even. Today I am happy being me!

ON THIS BOLD AND SASSY LAYOUT, Vicki layered bright patterned papers and placed three large but simple chipboard flowers as accents. The large title and bead-centered buttons both add extra elements of color and dimension. The resulting page is powerful—and it was completed in less than an hour.

{Me}
Vicki Boutin, Burlington, Ontario, Canada

SUPPLIES:

Patterned paper (Basic Grey, Scrapworks); chipboard flowers (Imagination Project); brackets (Heidi Swapp); metal letters (American Crafts); dye ink; buttons, ribbon (source unknown); pen

LISA CHOSE PINK AND BLACK to make a bold statement on this sweet layout. She used scalloped cardstock she gave the appearance of having spent time hand-cutting—even though she didn't. She accentuated the theme with a silk flower with a black center to bring the color forward and make the number "3" pop. To finish, she added a touch of sass by outlining the black title in white to make it stand out.

In Between
Lisa VanderVeen, Mendham, New Jersey

SUPPLIES:

Patterned paper (Bo-Bunny Press); circle punch (Creative Memories); flower (Heidi Swapp); stickers (American Craft); pen; cardstock

At almost 3, you are definitely in between.

Not a baby, not a girl.

Not independent, but wanting to do it all.

You still want your paci and blankie.

You aren't potty-trained.

You're still in a crib.

Definitely in between.

3

in between

When did my love for anything pink begin? I have no clue. I remember loving pink Barbie stuff, pink dresses, and pink birthday cakes as a child. Why do I love pink so much? That's an easy one. It makes me feel good. Pink candy, pink lipstick and fingernail polish, pink clothes, and pink walls. With two little girls who also love pink, the fun never ends! March 2006

THIS DESIGN'S HOT, HOT COLORS and patterns shout "sassy." Angelia fashioned her main floral accent in the style of the big brooches that are recurringly popular in the fashion world. Her colorful background is blocked with strips of white cardstock and with sequin trim added to the intersections. Chipboard letters construct a quick title, and her journaling, printed in pink, adds to the theme without requiring any extra assembly time.

Pink
Angelia Wigginton, Belmont, Mississippi

SUPPLIES:

Patterned paper (7 Gypsies); chipboard letters, photo corner, floral center sticker (Heidi Swapp); silver buckle (Li'l Davis Designs); sequin trim, pink crystals, silk flower (source unknown); Evergreen font (Two Peas in a Bucket)

THE MAGIC OF CHRISTMAS MORNING is joyfully depicted on Samuel's layout. A wealth of gemstones, glitter, stars, beads and baubles make this holiday page twinkle with color. Samuel used existing products in his scrapbook supply that are easy to apply to any page and that quickly add a little interest and pizzazz.

Christmas Morn
Samuel Cole, Stillwater, Minnesota

SUPPLIES:

Patterned paper (Chatterbox, Karen Foster Design, K & Company, KI Memories, Scenic Route Paper Co.); circle punch, vellum snowflakes (EK Success); epoxy stickers (Creative Imaginations); buttons, glitter, ribbon, gemstones (Paper Bliss); printed gift wrap tape (MJ Zoom); circle stamp (Hero Arts); glitter stickers (Me & My Big Ideas); charms (American Traditional Designs); stamping inks; circle cutter; corner rounder; star brads (Making Memories); typewriter stamp (JustRite Stampers); pen; cardstock

athlete
team player
YOU BETTER Believe IT
Athlete
DETERMINATION
Showing your stuff is not always consistent. Some days you're on, and some days you're not. Today, you packed the heat, and were right on the money!
3-5-2006
in training in training in training
got GAME?

URBAN

The urban style marches to a hip, irreverent beat. A mixture of grunge and graffiti, this style imparts a crude, rundown vibe while portraying spunk and tenacity. It can be macabre and gruesome without being gory or frightful. Common attributes include mesh, metals, dog tags, bottle caps, staples, brick wall backgrounds, ransom-style lettering, city backdrops and more (see page 9 for more information). The urban style is most often seen on masculine and teen pages, but this style can work for just about any theme if the materials and design are executed correctly. So get ready to get your grunge on!

URBAN Trademarks

COLOR

Color used on urban pages depends first and foremost on the photographs and theme, but often the shades that shine forth march to a masculine beat.

Masculine colors such as black, brown, blue and gray
Silver
Military colors
Bold colors such as red or orange

ACCENTS

No boundaries, no rules…the urban style revolutionizes the traditional layout with a mixture of daring elements that jump off the page.

Metal wire
Mesh
Embossed metal sheets
Metal mouldings
Large brads or grommets
Bottle caps
Dog tags
Metal hinges
Sand
Corrugated paper

PATTERNS

Much like the graphic style, patterns tend to be minimal in the urban mode. However, they can serve to accent gripping photos and unique type treatments that are the hallmarks of this style. Here are some common patterns you'll hit upon when creating urban pages.

Brick wall backgrounds
Graffiti or city backgrounds
Large, unique shapes
Stripes
Camouflage or military

Ginger

Traci

Barb

Kelly

FOUR WOMEN
TEN CHILDREN
FIVE COLLEGE DEGREES
TWO BRUNETTES
ONE BLONDE
ONE RED HEAD
TWO TEACHERS
ONE LIBRARIAN
ONE ENGINEER
ONE CREATIVE DIRECTOR

TWO ARTISTS
THREE JOCKS
TWO BLACK BELTS
ONE PAPER DESIGNER
ONE FLUENT IN FRENCH
ONE MOTHER OF TWINS
FOUR VACATION LOVERS
FOUR INTO GREYS
ANATOMY

MY BEST
FRIENDS....

DESPERATE
HOUSEWIVES

A BLACK-AND-WHITE PHOTO of four fabulous ladies striking a pose is the main focal point on this tongue-in-cheek layout. Spoofing the popular prime-time soap series *Desperate Housewives*, Barb uses list-style journaling to show how these ladies are anything but. A gray background, large silver brads and ransom-style lettering induce a grungy feel, while large chipboard letters inked in black balance the bottom half of the page.

Desperate Housewives
Barb Hogan, Cincinnati, Ohio

SUPPLIES:

Patterned paper (Diane's Daughters, SEI); brads (Making Memories); chipboard letters (Li'l Davis Designs); ink; pen; font (Two Peas in a Bucket)

FIVE 5 FIVE

&

ONE ONE ONE 1 8

Cousins

DREW & MELODEE

Both are an only child

Both have blonde hair

One lives in Michigan

One lives in Arkansas

One is five years old and just starting school

One is eighteen and about to graduate high school

They share a special bond

Both are a little bit spoiled

Both are very loved

#1234567890

favorite

OFFICIALLY ADORABLE OFFICIALLY

MELODEE EFFECTIVELY ILLUSTRATES here how a tender photo can work with the grunge style. She stamped her journaling onto the inked cardstock background to give the layout a bit of a distressed feel. To keep it quick and easy, she used only one style of patterned paper on the right side of the layout. She used a distressed-looking font and adhered bold epoxy numbers to carry out the metro, urban feel of the layout while doubling as a title.

5 & 18
Melodee Langworthy, Rockford, Michigan

SUPPLIES:

Patterned paper, epoxy stickers (Creative Imaginations); rub-ons (7 Gypsies, Creative Imaginations, Scenic Route Paper Co.); arrow (EK Success); tag (Making Memories); stamps (Limited Edition Rubberstamps); stamping ink; Dirty Ego, Adler fonts (Dafont)

TO CREATE A GRUNGE-STYLE LOOK on this layout honoring her loving husband, Holly selected coordinating papers with heavily inked edges and used staples and brads to adhere the mesh metal background and vellum journaling strips. She chose a selection of metal and "urban" fonts to enhance the theme. She also cut a metal frame in half, inked the edges with black and used it as a metal photo corner.

Father of the Year
Holly Corbett, Central, South Carolina

SUPPLIES:

Patterned paper (Basic Grey); brads, metal screen, metal washers, metal frame, tags, chain, metal circle letters (Making Memories); nameplate (Magic Scraps); file folders (Rusty Pickle); letter stamps (FontWerks); chipboard letters (Li'l Davis Designs); chalk ink; vellum; solvent ink; staples; cardstock

A THRILLING SKATEBOARD STUNT is caught on film in this urban-style layout. Kim converted her main action photo to black-and-white and blew it up for a big impact. She easily distressed it by dipping the edge of a plastic ruler in black paint and then repeatedly pressing the ruler edge against the photo. To add authenticity to the page, she printed skater lingo on colored paper and cut it into strips.

Skate
Kim Kesti, Phoenix, Arizona

SUPPLIES:

Patterned paper, letter stickers (Scrapworks); brads (Happy Hammer); acrylic paint (Making Memories); stamping ink; SP Coffee Break font (Scrapworks)

Traveling down Route 66 brings me back to my childhood and road trips with my family. Dad would drive, mom would navigate, and us kids would mostly sleep.

When we were young, my folks would put the back seat of the station wagon down and Lorri and I would stretch out with our blankets and pillows, drifting in and out of sleep as the engine hummed beneath us and the miles fell behind.

We'd always ask, "How much further?" How much further to the next gas station? How much further until the next state line? How much further until we stopped at a rest stop for lunch? How much further until we found a roadside motel with a swimming pool and a vibrating bed to stop at for the night? How much further until the final destination?

Grandma Link made us travel boxes with games, playing cards, and snacks. Candy was a special treat when we were kids, but grandma put enough in our boxes to last the whole trip if we were careful. We'd sing made-up songs and count out-of-state license plates to pass the time.

We never had new cars when I was a kid. I remember lots of breakdowns and small-town garages. There were times when we had to wait for parts to come in before we could continue on our journey. When I was about ten, we bought a camper. Lorri,

Scott, and I would watch the world go by from the window in the overhead or pass the time with card games at the camper's table. Climbing through the window to snuggle between my parents in the truck was a special opportunity offered rarely and only to one child at a time. Sometimes we'd stop at a KOA, but we'd usually get a motel room so we'd have a place to shower. When I was in high school, our family bought a twelve-passenger van. Each of us kids had our own seat to stretch out and sleep on.

We'd have breakfast at small cafes and eat dinner at truck stops. To save money, we'd never order a drink or dessert. For lunch, we'd stop at a local grocery store and buy fixings for sandwiches to eat at a scenic overlook or at a historical marker.

Flash forward thirty-five years. I am married with two boys of my own. Our family has jetted all over the world and cruised the Caribbean, but we were missing the nostalgia of our own childhood road trips. It didn't seem right that our boys had been to Buenos Aires and Paris, but had never seen the Grand Canyon. We bought a National Parks Pass and vowed to see as many as we could.

We now take a road trip at least once a year. We'll usually head to a National Park over either Fall Break or Spring Break. Either one of these times can be a bit chilly, but we have discovered that the parks are a lot less crowded. We've been to Arches, Bryce Canyon, Zion, Rocky Mountain National Park, Mesa Verde, Mount Rushmore, the Petrified Forest, and the Grand Canyon. We'd like to go to Yosmite and Yellowstone.

We put the back seat in the van down and pile the space with gear. John does most of the driving, but I lack the skills needed to be a good navigator. Eric and Kevin each have their own captain's chair in the middle row of the van. We like to listen to books on tape. We'll try and spot out-of-state license plates plates and make up funny songs. We'll use the letters on license plates to come up with goofy sayings. We brainstorm possible band names. We talk about the features that our dream homes would have. We haven't bought a DVD player for the car because it would disconnect us frm each other. The boys sleep a bit. I sleep a bit.

I enjoy this family time. Long hours in the car to talk to each other. Sleeping in hotel rooms. We don't stop at the roadside attractions very often, but the boys don't seem to mind. The trips are as much about the journey as the destination.

These photos were taken on a recent drive through New Mexico and Arizona on our way to the Grand Canyon. One of the ways we entertained ourselves on the drive was by spotting the old Route 66 signs and establishments. I'd have my camera ready and try to capture the nostalgic signs as we sped past at 80mph. John and I told the boys about the road trips we'd taken as kids. We'd reminisce about our childhood memories as we made new memories with our own children.

KELLI'S ROAD TRIP with her family along famed Route 66 is happily depicted in this photo montage. While her journaling serves as an entertaining travel diary, it is the sequence of photos that takes you on the real adventure. She painted the transparency and then trimmed it with a die-cut machine to create her title and custom-made Route 66 sign. The distressed background paper and the look of peeling creates an urban feel perfect for a page on this theme.

Get Your Kicks Route 66
Kelli Noto, Centennial, Colorado

SUPPLIES:

Image-editing software (Adobe); patterned paper (Karen Foster Design); acrylic paint; transparency; die-cut letters (QuicKutz)

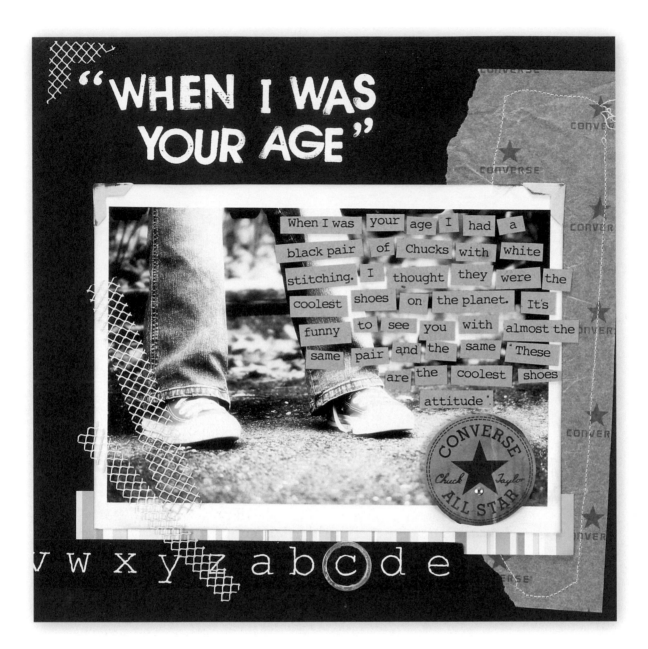

"WHEN I WAS YOUR AGE"

When I was your age I had a black pair of Chucks with white stitching. I thought they were the coolest shoes on the planet. It's funny to see you with almost the same pair and the same "These are the coolest shoes attitude".

v w x y z a b c d e

MARIE DECIDED TO USE a large photo as her focal point in this grafitti-style layout. Journaling broken into mini strips, metal mesh and a metal washer all give it a grunge feel. The photo of the teen's shoes plays upon the universal popularity of sneakers among teens of every generation. Tissue paper from the original packaging is stitched on the right side to help balance the page.

When I Was Your Age
Marie Cox, Springfield, Massachusetts

SUPPLIES:

Patterned paper (Autumn Leaves); metal mesh, metal tag (Making Memories); rhinestone, photo corners (Heidi Swapp); letter stamps (Educational Insights); gaffer tape (7 Gypsies); tissue paper; cardstock

KELLI SCRATCHED HER PHOTO and sanded her transparency to lend a grunge feel to this dare devil layout. She created a clever lettering technique by using a die-cut machine to cut letters from a plastic milk bottle. An old window screen adhered with black brads provides a textured background. All of these "trash" elements are turned to treasure in this urban design.

Freefalling
Kelli Noto, Centennial, Colorado
Photo: Michael Smith, Aurora, Colorado

SUPPLIES:

Image-editing software (Adobe); die-cut letters and arrow (QuicKutz); brads (Happy Hammer); window screen; plastic milk carton; transparency; cardstock

Kevin loved the feeling of freefalling. He had a huge smile on his face the entire time. We went to an indoor skydiving place where you can ride on a column of air and experience freefall. The instructor helped Kevin get his positioning and then let him go. The skydiving picture seemed incongruent with the folding chairs that you could see through the chamber's glass panes, so I used Photoshop to add Kevin's picture to a photo that my dad had of some clouds. You didn't think I was crazy enough to actually let my son jump out of an airplane, did you? Even if Kevin really did go skydiving, I would never jump out of an airplane after him--not even for a once-in-a-lifetime photo! Kevin thinks that he'd like to his birthday party at the same place. He also thinks he wants to try skydiving for real. UH-OH!

FREEFALLING

FUN + FUNKY

Do you like to mix and match bright colors and patterns? Do your pages flaunt a festive flair? Splashy, hip and a little retro, the fun and funky style has something for everyone. The pages that follow sport free-form abstract shapes and curves, fun and unusual color choices, hand-drawn elements, and designs and patterns inspired by past decades as well as modern pop culture (see page 10 for more details). This chapters brims with fresh inspiration and eye-popping design options for creating carefree pages that set a fun and funky mood.

FUN + FUNKY

COLOR

Fun and funky pages often have a lot going on, so color play is a must for this style. Don't be afraid to whip out that color wheel and experiment with split complemenary, diad, triad, and tetrad color schemes. A rainbow of groovy color possibilities awaits you. Here are some ideas you'll see on the pages that follow.

Bright colors such as hot pink, bright orange and fire-engine red
Retro colors such as aqua, pink, yellow and green
Colors taken from popular ads and other media

ACCENTS

Add flavor to your pages with a pinch of whimsy and dash of fancy. The fun and funky style incorporates a variety of traditional items and textures that can be used in new-fangled ways. Here are just a few that you'll see in this chapter.

Doodles
Fabric
Paper shapes and strips
Chipboard shapes and letters
Silk flowers
Buttons
Faux stitching
Tags

PATTERNS

Call upon the power of patterns when crafting fun and funky pages. With an endless array of papers to choose from, your only challenge will be narrowing down your selection. Remember to coordinate colors and prints effectively to achieve a cohesive look.

Abstract and freestyle shapes
Flowers
Polka dots
Stars
Lettering or newspaper print

VICKI PULLED OUT HER colored pencils and created this completely loose and "doodled" page full of charisma and charm. She used pens to draw the vine and part of the title. Vicki says she had no rhyme or reason; she just worked it out as she went along. She then quickly added some color to the drawing and a little ink to the rest of the page. The entire process took less than an hour to complete.

Love You, Devyn
Vicki Boutin, Burlington, Ontario, Canada

SUPPLIES:

Patterned paper (Imagination Project, Sassafras Lass); rub-ons (Imagination Project); dye ink; colored pencils; pens

TO CREATE A FUN AND FUNKY PAGE, you need fun and funky photos! Jessie got her lil' sis to model some goofy poses in what appears to have been an amusing photo shoot. When creating the page, Jessie randomly adhered strips of colored cardstock, added the priceless photos and drew a variety of doodles. She says the whole page came together in a jiff.

Liane
Jessie Baldwin, Las Vegas, Nevada

SUPPLIES:

Rickrack (Doodlebug Design); black gel pen; white pen; cardstock

THIS BRIGHT AND BOLD PAGE features Shannon with her cropping comrades—an online group otherwise known as Funky Fresh Flavor. Because this patterned paper is so funky on its own, Shannon wanted to create a clean, flat layout that was simple and free of too many embellishments. She positioned the stars to "shoot" out of the photo, which is filled with her superstar friends. Sticker letters and handwritten journaling complete the page.

Funky Fresh Flavor
Shannon Taylor, Bristol, Tennessee

SUPPLIES:

Patterned paper (SEI); letter stickers (Chatterbox); black pen (Zig)

DEB SAW THE "UMBRELLA" in this photo as an opportunity to create a big, bold design theme that was funky and playful. She simply used tracing paper to trace the shape of the umbrella in the original photo, transferred the image onto paper and fabric, and then cut it out and added it to the layout. She finished by adding a few star stickers, a metal tag and chain and handwritten journaling over the photo. Totally cool and totally easy!

As If
Deb Perry, Newport News, Virginia

SUPPLIES:

Patterned paper (7 Gypsies, Imagination Project; K & Company, Karen Foster Design); metal tag, stickers (Mrs. Grossman's); stitching (K & Company); fabric (Jo-Ann Stores); rub-on letters (Imagination Project); brad (Karen Foster Design); white pen

RENEE WANTED TO CREATE a page with freestyle elements, doodles and lots of prints and textures. Using strips of patterned paper and decorative scissors was an easy way to add color and a sense of movement to the page. For the title, she combined chipboard letters and a funky font that she printed and trimmed out of cardstock. Flowers cut out of patterned paper make cute and practically effortless accents. And the hand-drawn doodling on the photo bestows a unique feel to the whole piece.

Princess Smarty Pants
Renee Coffey, Auburn, Georgia

SUPPLIES:

Patterned paper (Anna Griffin, KI Memories, SEI); chipboard letters (Heidi Swapp); chipboard flower (KI Memories); epoxy sticker (MOD); cardstock; decorative scissors; Tokyo Girl font (Two Peas in a Bucket)

VICKI CHOSE A FITTING '50S THEME for this retro page. She achieved the look of the era by using a pink, aqua and yellow color scheme that is a true representation of the style of the decade. The curved, free-form shape in the background was inspired by a vintage ad, and the star paper, retro stamps and chipboard sign complete the look. She kept the page simple, using a few key design elements and materials to make it shine.

Beach Babe
Vicki Boutin, Burlington, Ontario, Canada

SUPPLIES:

Patterned paper (Imagination Project, SEI); chipboard sign (Li'l Davis Designs); stamps (Scraptivity); solvent ink; brads (Making Memories); cardstock; pen

At first you were cautious. Not too sure what to make of this new experience. Was it supposed to be fun or just messy? After some careful consideration you came to the conclusion that the beach was fun and you started to dig in. Once you were at ease you made for quite the Beach Babe!!!!

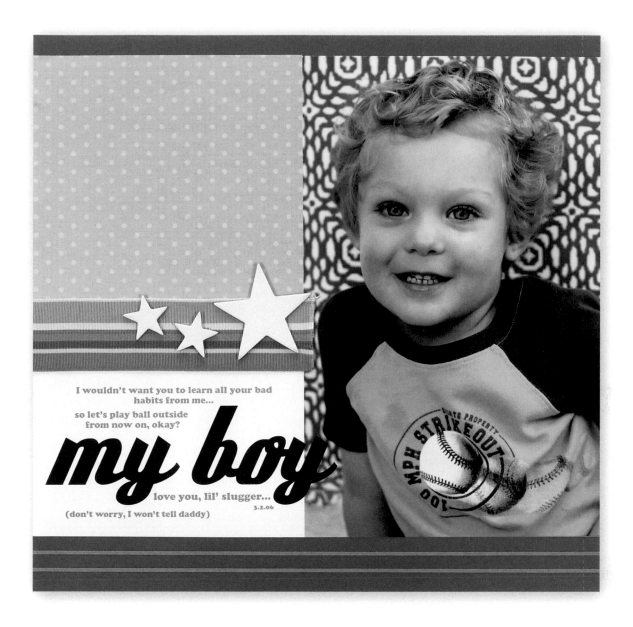

I wouldn't want you to learn all your bad habits from me...

so let's play ball outside from now on, okay?

my boy

love you, lil' slugger...

(don't worry, I won't tell daddy)

3.2.06

FOR THIS TIMELESS PAGE featuring her little baseball star, Joanna chose to use a combination of colors and fonts she associates with the retro style. Mini polka dots, striped ribbon and the white chipboard stars in particular reminded her of the popular TV shows of the '70s and '80s. The page came together quickly and easily because it employs minimal paper and embellishments. According to Joanna, the most tedious task was creating and arranging the text boxes. She says, "Once that's done, everything else falls into place."

My Boy
Joanna Bolick, Fletcher, North Carolina

SUPPLIES:

Patterned paper (Chatterbox, Heidi Swapp); chipboard stars (Heidi Swapp); ribbon (Strano Designs); cardstock; Cooper, Deftone Stylus fonts

In 1977, at age 16, I sure thought I was super foxy in my slippery, polyester blouse and Farrah Fawcett flip hairdo. Can you dig it, baby?

That TORREY Chick

TORREY RE-CREATED A VINTAGE '70s floral design she found on the Internet by trimming it out of cardstock. She used a circle cutting system to ensure the beige outline would be uniform. The teenage photo of Torrey shown here had turned red-orange over time, as many photos of that era have. Instead of correcting it in a photo-editing program, she decided to leave it that funky orange color to add authenticity to the layout. She also chose fonts of the period to create her title—a spoof on the popular *That '70s Show*—which is cut from cardstock.

That Torrey Chick
Torrey Scott, Thornton, Colorado

SUPPLIES:

Patterned paper (Die Cuts With A View); foam spacers; circle punch, corner rounder (FK Success); Magic Matter; circle cutting system (Creative Memories); cardstock

GRETA USED SLICES OF BRIGHT ORANGE and funky green to add a retro zest to her page chronicling her childhood years in the '70s. She used a color-blocking technique with just a few touches of detail, such as her chipboard flower and free-form swoosh, to give the page visual interest. This allowed for a no-fuss design. Retro printed paper, a '70s style font and rounded corners complete the authentic look.

70's Girl
Greta Hammond, Goshen, Indiana
Photo: Bonnie Miller, McPherson, Kansas

SUPPLIES:

Patterned paper (Die Cuts With A View); chipboard flower (Fancy Pants); brads (Making Memories); cardstock; Candice font (Scrapvillage)

Born in 1971, I am a 70's girl. Although still a young girl, I remember so many of the styles that were prevalent during that decade. The halter tops, the terry cloth jump suits, the tube tops - we had it all. But even more than just clothing styles was the feeling of the 70's. We were carefree kids, roaming the neighborhood on our bikes and roller skates. We spent hours and hours down by the pond exploring and just being kids. It was certainly a different time but one that I won't forget anytime soon.

70's Girl

kate

What is my
little girl made of?

Polly Pocket, Winx Club,
High Honor Roll, SEARCH, chapter
books, saving for shoes, blue Doritos,
Taco Bell, shakin' her booty, wishing for a
friend, trying to be good. My little girl is made
up of wishes and dreams and sweetness. I
love you, Katelyn, with all my heart!

you

A few of my
favorite things

XO XO XO XO XO XO XO XO XO XO XO

JENNIFER CREATED THIS FAVORITES PAGE utilizing a retro color scheme. She began by trimming a large circle from brown cardstock and placing all of her supporting elements on the circle before adhering it onto a green background. The color scheme is unusual but works well, creating a warm glow to match her daughter's beautiful face. A hot pink flower introduces a burst of eye-pleasing brightness.

A Few of My Favorite Things
Jennifer Gallacher, Savannah, Georgia

SUPPLIES:

Patterned paper (Déjà Views, Provo Craft); chipboard letters, scrapper's tape, ribbon (Li'l Davis Designs); sentiment rub-on (Déjà Views); snaps (Making Memories); photo corners (Canson); acrylic word circle (KI Memories); stamps (Karen Foster Design); stamping ink; acrylic heart (Heidi Grace Designs); silk flower (Heidi Swapp); cardstock; font SP You've Got Mail (Scrapsupply)

RETRO DESIGN ELEMENTS and the light green, aqua and yellow color palette work together on Marie's toddler page. The paper designs mimic children's book illustrations and lend a fun and funky feel. Marie wanted to keep her approach simple so she kept the remaining elements—a chipboard title and computer-generated journaling block—to a minimum.

18 Months
Marie Cox, Springfield, Massachusetts

SUPPLIES:

Paper designs (Jen Harrison); chipboard letters and numbers, photo corners (Heidi Swapp); cardstock

months

18

At 18 months you are starting to assert yourself. Your personality is slowly coming out and you are learning more each day. You love to copy your brother and sister and we all get a kick out of your budding language skills. Sometimes we have to guess at what your saying. You enjoy dancing to music and playing your bongo drums for daddy. I can't wait to see how much you change in 18 more months.

Whenever Kiersten and Chloe get together you can hear

nothing but giggles! They seem to laugh at just about

anything and keep themselves and those around them

well entertained! Love these two girls so much!

~April 2006

IF YOU'RE IN NEED OF SOME INSPIRATION, ads and Web sites can be great sources, as Heather proves in this humorous piece. She got her general design concept and color scheme from a Sam's Club logo, but added her own unique spin to it by featuring the photo of the giggly girls acting goofy. The geometric shapes provide the perfect photo mats, while strips of journaling adhered with multi-colored brads share the story behind the cheesy-toothed tykes.

Giggly Girls
Heather Preckel, Swannanoa, North Carolina

SUPPLIES:

Brads (Junkitz); heart button (source unknown); cardstock; font Flower Pot (Two Peas in a Bucket)

JESSIE WANTED TO CREATE A PAGE that loosely mimics a Coke bottle without using the exact brand logo. Creating the patterned paper swirl at the bottom of the page proved to be the perfect solution. She used a standard hole punch to construct the white circle "bubbles" and included fancy rub-ons as her own creative touch. A handy die-cut machine made creating the title a cinch.

He's the Real Thing
Jessie Baldwin, Las Vegas, Nevada

SUPPLIES:

Patterned paper, rub-ons (Basic Grey); brads (American Crafts); die-cut letters (Sizzix); white pen; cardstock

KELLI WAS INSPIRED by popular iPod advertisements to create an iconic photo collage on this page. To achieve the hip photo effect, she shot pictures of her young friend dancing in silhouette and then darkened the images in Photoshop while placing bright colors in the background. A simple journaling block and white title letters are the only additions needed to complete this exuberant page.

Playlist
Kelli Noto, Centennial, Colorado

SUPPLIES:

Image-editing software
(Adobe); die-cut letters
(QuicKutz); cardstock

PLAYLIST

Alison changes the tunes on her iPod about once a month. During the month of April, 2006, she had Carrie Underwood, Martina McBride, Maroon 5, Bo Bice, Green Day, Gwen Stepani, Shakira, and Kenny Chesney on her playlist. Her iPod will hold about a 1,000 songs, but she only has it half full. She'll listen to it in the car and while she is doing her homework. We've even had to take it away from her after she has fallen asleep!

JULY 2005

Love me, love my dog!!

When I got Frankie as a gift

for my 40th birthday I was head over

heels in love at first sight!! He is such

a sweet little dog and who could resist that

adorable face!!! If you are going to hang

around with me...you really

MUST love Dogs

KATHY LOVES HER PUP, and anyone who spends time at her home better love him, too. The free-form shapes and large curves keep the feel of this page funky and fresh. The title, taken from the popular movie, finishes the journaling, which is made from free-cut white cardstock. The cut pieces of ribbon, rub-ons and large accents all make this layout quick and easy to put together.

Must Love Dogs
Kathy Fesmire, Athens, Tennessee

SUPPLIES:

Patterned paper (Basic Grey, My Mind's Eye); bone accents (Wrights); sticker letters (Doodlebug Designs); rub-ons (Making Memories; My Mind's Eye); ribbon (Offray); heart (Wal-Mart); stamping ink; cardstock

in sunshine and shade in sunshine and shade

friends always offer gas money
friends buy you silly slippers for no reason
friends are always willing to pose for photos
friends don't mind trying new things

friends don't care if you buy the same clothes
friends aren't perfect
friends know you aren't perfect
friends are forever

friends sing along
friends are always there for you
friends in sunshine
friends in shade

dana, meghan, nicki – 02/06

A BLACK-AND-WHITE PHOTO paired with a trio of color composes this fun teen page. Kim manipulated her photo in Photoshop to add a "pop art" feel to the lay-out. She first turned the photo to black-and-white, then experimented with the "contrast" tool until she achieved the effect she desired and finished by printing it onto a transparency. A pinwheel of red, orange and blue sits atop a white background in the upper left corner and provides the right amount of punch to keep the layout vibrant and colorful.

In Sunshine and Shade
Kim Kesti, Phoenix, Arizona

SUPPLIES:

Image-editing software (Adobe); patterned paper (Autumn Leaves, Cherry Arte); textured cardstock (Canson); brads (Bazzill); transparency ; stamping ink; cardstock

LOOKING TO THE *TV Guide* lineup for a little inspiration, Barb was able to play off the theme of a popular show, *My Name Is Earl*, while adding her own unique twist. She used coordinating patterned papers and printed computer-generated journaling to pull this page together fast. Type placed strategically on curves as well as repeated circle elements add movement and energy to the page. The journaling list, a take off on Earl's "list," is printed in a childlike font on crumpled notebook paper to mimic a child's handwritten to-do list.

My Name Is Shannon
Barb Hogan, Cincinnati, Ohio

SUPPLIES:

Patterned paper, rub-ons, die-cut flower and letters (Imagination Project); pin (Prym-Dritz); buttons (Hobby Lobby); stamping ink; pen; cardstock; font (Two Peas in a Bucket)

beautiful

its true

you make our lives

more beautiful

2004

{sydney}

romantic

Do you fall in love with soft pastels, pretty florals, delicate trimmings of lace and layer after layer of texture? Are you seduced by sumptuous patterns, lovely textiles and carefully chosen accents and embellishments? Don't be afraid to let the romantic style enchant you with its sophistication and elegance. Upon first glance this style may daunt beginners, but with a little imagination, ingenuity and inspiration, you too can create beautiful scrapbook pages reflective of this graceful art. Be enticed by the artistic variations of this style, including trés chic, French country, distressed and Bohemian (see page 11 for detailed information). Each offers its own unique characteristics and scores of artistic possibilities.

romantic Trademarks

COLOR

The romantic style can blush with pretty pinks or glow with rich browns and golds. Color choice will depend upon the mood you want to convey and the particular style you lean toward.

Trés chic colors such as white, pink or other colors in the pastel family
French country colors such as red, cinnamon, auburn, green and blue
Antique colors such as brown, tan, taupe and russet
Bohemian colors such as purple, brown and burgandy

ACCENTS

The romantic category boasts the most embellishments and textures. Layer after layer, you'll find an endless supply of elements to add richness and flavor to these beautiful pages.

Lace
Fabric including toile, velvet, felt, burlap and calico
Ribbon, rickrack and fibers
Pressed flowers and leaves
Silk and paper flowers
Buttons
Chicken wire
Wooden accents
Crackled wood
Distressed paint

PATTERNS

Patterns play an important role in the romantic category because they must perfectly blend to create a unified whole. Fortunately, with so many paper possiblities, the combinations are endless.

Flowers
Polka dots
Harlequins
Hearts
Gingham
Stripes
Contemporary shapes and designs

Grace and Monica, I love it when you come over to my house to play. You are so sweet and innocent. Child's Play. It is absolutely precious!

precious

"OH SO PRETTY" are words that come to mind to describe the beauty of this layout. To create it in a simple and fast way, Sharon cut strips of different papers to use as her base and then dry-brushed all of them at once with white paint. The stamped title letters and all of the embellishments were painted a simple white as well. This white-washed look—mixed with the pink, brown and white color palette and a few romantic embellishments—truly makes this layout "trés chic."

Precious
Sharon Laakkonen, Superior, Wisconsin

SUPPLIES:

Patterned paper (Chatterbox, Imagination Project, Scenic Route Paper Co.); chipboard letters (Heidi Swapp); fabric (MaisyMo Designs); mini brads (Queen & Co.); swirl stamp (Wildflower Stamps); paper flowers (Prima); metal photo corners (Frost Creek Charms); lace, rickrack (source unknown); distress ink; acrylic paint; pen; thread

TWO

Once Upon a Time

No matter how much you two fuss, fight, or argue, there are times when there is nothing better than a playmate, a buddy, a sister. This was such a day. Puddles to be splashed in, mud to be played in and memories to be made.   Olivia and Michaela, 10 and 6 April 2006

GOOD TIMES

THIS LAYOUT is all about textures and rich details. For a distressed look, Angelia lightly scruffed the edges of her patterned paper blocks and added pale pink ink to the edges. She added visual interest with lace, a button, a pearl and silver brad, metal photo turns and a black metal accent. The heavy chipboard letters combined with a rub-on phrase make a quick and easy title that doesn't look like a shortcut.

Two
Angelia Wigginton, Belmont, Mississippi

SUPPLIES:

Patterned paper, metal plate, photo turns (7 Gypsies); chipboard letters, lace, flower, button (source unknown); cardstock

THESE SOFT, ROMANTIC PAPERS and the pink, blue and yellow color palette are perfect for this style. Trudy layered her patterned papers and lace to create a quick and attractive foundation. She chose three striking black-and-white photos ideal for this type of page. Flowers are the perfect way to maintain balance by pulling color to various parts of the page while re-enforcing the theme set by the papers and hanging baskets in the focal photo. Distressed chipboard letters and rub-ons make for an easy title.

Far & Away Cousins
Trudy Sigurdson, Victoria, British Columbia, Canada

SUPPLIES:

Patterned paper (Autumn Leaves); chipboard monogram, silk flower (Heidi Swapp); chipboard letters (Making Memories); paper flowers (Prima); brads, stamping ink (Bazzill); photo anchors (7 Gypsies); die-cut letters and flourishes (QuicKutz); lace (source unknown)

eyes so
blue

Betsy has the most startling blue eyes - she is a true princess in the family. All she needs to do is turn on those beautiful baby blues.
~ nov. 2005 ~

PRETTY AS A PRINCESS, the baby featured on this layout is sure to steal your heart. Kim chose the perfect papers and accents to adorn her treasured photo. She painted the chipboard letters, then lightly sanded the edges with an emery board to give the whole layout a trés chic feel. The use of baby-soft colors, buttons, rickrack and ribbon adds to the theme. Handwritten journaling provides the perfect finishing touch.

Eyes So Blue
Kim Kesti, Phoenix, Arizona

SUPPLIES

Patterned paper, chipboard letters, rub-on letters, photo corners (Imagination Project); buttons (Junkitz); lace trim (Wrights); ribbon (May Arts); transparency (Creative Imaginations); cardstock

PRETTY PASTELS and flirty flowers inspired Courtney to create this page highlighting the arrival of spring. She layered her papers and added some simple texture with rickrack and velvet letter stickers for her title. To keep the page quick and easy, she chose papers with printed stitching, giving the look of being hand-sewn but requiring far less work. Paper flowers accented with buttons complement the precious photo.

Spring
Courtney Walsh, Winnebago, Illinois

SUPPLIES:

Patterned paper (Junkitz); buttons (FoofaLa); embroidery floss (DMC); letter stickers (Making Memories); rickrack (Wrights); cardstock

Sitting outside in short sleeves after a long winter.
Soaking up sunshine as the days grow longer.
Coolish breeze messing up your hair.
Bikes, balls, grass, dirt... Spring is finally here.
I love watching you get rid of that cabin fever once and for all!

THERE'S NOTHING MORE ROMANTIC than romance itself. Suzy chose these photos of a blissful bride and groom to create a trés chic page complete with pastel colors and vintage papers. She used pre-made metal photo corners that are lightly distressed to allow the silver to shine through, and dry-brushed a band of white paint to border the top and bottom of the layout. Sheer polka-dot ribbon and mini paper flowers add a dash of delight to this heavenly page.

Eternal Love
Suzy Plantamura, Laguna Niguel, California

SUPPLIES:

Patterned paper, letter stickers, metal photo corners, ribbon, acrylic paint (Making Memories); rub-on circle (K & Company); paper flowers (Prima); pen

as I took pictures at Jennie and Todd's wedding, I was amazed and touched by the look of love on their faces. To be so young and find etenal love is truly a dream come true. Suzy - March 2006

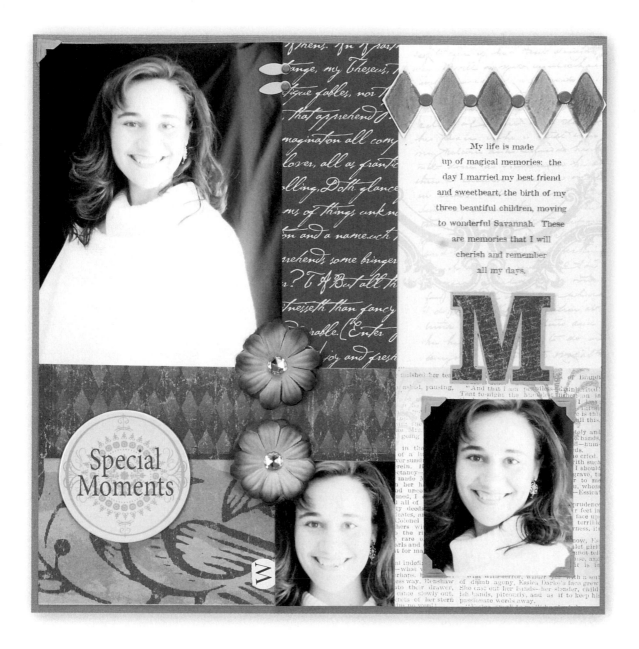

My life is made up of magical memories: the day I married my best friend and sweetheart, the birth of my three beautiful children, moving to wonderful Savannah. These are memories that I will cherish and remember all my days.

Special Moments

MOMENTS AND MEMORIES are the themes of Jennifer's warmhearted page. She chose to mix papers printed with a variety of words and patterns to create a color-blocked design. Chipboard elements, purple snaps and silk flowers accented with large rhinestones add a textural quality, while a trio of photos printed in sepia showcase the artist herself. Using a variety of pre-made items kept the page quick and easy.

Special Moments
Jennifer Gallacher, American Fork, Utah

SUPPLIES:

Patterned paper (Autumn Leaves, Creative Imaginations, Déjà Views); photo turns, purple brads (Junkitz); photo corners (Canson); silk flowers, chipboard circle (Li'l Davis Designs); letter tab (Autumn Leaves); diamond stamp, snaps (Making Memories); monogram "M" (Déjà Views); acrylic paint; cardstock

КУРИЦА

It's pronounced *KOO-ree-tzah* and it means "chicken" in Russian. Every time I see a chicken, I think of the Russian word for it. Why? Well, I studied Russian for 4 years in school, and though most of my vocabulary has slipped into oblivion, a few words remain ...and **КУРИЦА** is one of them. I can also remember how to say *"The teacher stands near the window and writes on the chalkboard with chalk"* in Russian. Although I don't often have call to use it, it sounds REALLY impressive when I do.

TO CREATE THIS COUNTRY folk art page, Torrey started with a distressed-looking patterned paper for her background, then stenciled the chickens, wheat and chicken-footprint border with acrylic paint—a quick and easy technique that she says took less than ten minutes. She then sanded the close-up photo and distressed it with ink to match the overall feel. Torn gingham fabric tied in a bow completes the look.

КУРИЦА
Torrey Scott, Thornton, Colorado

SUPPLIES:

Patterned paper (Basic Grey); rivets (Making Memories); stencils (Plaid); distress ink; acrylic paint; fabric; sandpaper; transparency film; cardstock

THIS FRENCH COUNTRY PAGE featuring a loving grandmother and a giddy granddaughter gave Courtney the chance to experiment with mixing reds, yellows and blues as well as patterns in her papers. She trimmed the papers into blocks and strips and then layered them in a cohesive manner. Courtney says that even though it might look complicated, it really is easy to do. To finish, she added a few metal embellishments, a letter sticker title and journaling printed into strips.

Grammy's Girl
Courtney Walsh, Winnebago, Illinois

SUPPLIES:

Patterned paper (7 Gypsies, Anna Griffin, Chatterbox, Rusty Pickle); letter stickers (Scrapworks); metal snap (K & Company); metal brad (Making Memories); metal tag (Karen Russell)

FLORALS, STRIPES AND DIAMOND SHAPES harmonize to create a backdrop for Diana's endearing black-and-white photo of two young friends. To save time, she used a collection of coordinating patterned papers and opted for machine stitching instead of hand stitching. She also created the tags with stamps, rub-ons and her computer rather than making her own with layers of patterned paper, fabrics, trim and stitching. Fabric-covered buttons from her stash of scrapbook supplies add the perfect finishing touch to red silk flowers, and chipboard letters of three varieties compose the title.

Quite a Pair
Diana Hudson, Bakersfield, California

SUPPLIES:

Patterned paper (Bo-Bunny Press, Daisy D's, FoofaLa); flowers (Heidi Swapp); motif rub-on (Autumn Leaves); script stamp (Inkadinkado); chipboard letters (Making Memories, Pressed Petals); buttons (Prym-Dritz); ribbon (Offray); shipping tags (source unknown); fabric

Well, they're quite a pair but not like you might think. They look alike and they sometimes dress alike, but that's just about where the similarities end. Michelle is not the least bit shy and Sydney is pretty quiet until you get to know her. But when they are together, watch out!

True ♥ Love

George Abbott Mason & Lorraine Killingsworth

♥ August 25, 1944 ♥

Met in California. He was 11 years
her senior. Raised two little girls,
Gretchen & Virginia. Retired
together in Palm Desert, CA.

FOR THIS TOUCHING HERITAGE PAGE,
Shannon chose four different patterned
papers printed with vintage-looking designs.
She layered and inked the edges of each piece
to give them an aged appearance. She chose
a pre-made distressed wooden title and used
brads with heritage-style letters to further
play upon the theme. Handwritten journaling
relays all the important details to keep the
legacy of the couple alive for years to come.

True Love
Shannon Taylor, Bristol, Tennessee

SUPPLIES:

Patterned paper, twill
(FoofaLa); letter brads
(K & Company); title
letters, heart (We R
Memory Keepers);
stamping ink; black
pen

She's three

FOR THIS LAYOUT celebrating a little youngster turning three, Kathleen chose several patterned papers that fit in the French country theme, some of which already had a distressed, white-washed look. She simply cut strips of the different papers and put them together horizontally, then adhered ribbons, rickrack, lace and other notions to enhance the look. She used white acrylic paint on the metal embellishments and also to create the title from basic foam stamps. A scripty font chronicles the exciting day in Kathleen's journaling block.

She's Three
Kathleen Summers, Roseville, California

SUPPLIES:

Patterned paper (Foofala, My Mind's Eye); printed twill (Autumn Leaves); paper flowers (Chatterbox); foam letter stamps, brads, rickrack (Making Memories); metal pinwheels (American Tag); number stamp (Hero Arts); acrylic paint; jewelry tag, white mini brads (source unknown)

THE WARMTH AND CHARM of a New Zealand bed-and-breakfast is documented on Becky's inviting layout. She started by crumpling her patterned paper to give it a weathered look. She then sanded the edges of most of the elements and frayed the fabric strips. Pre-made embellishments and letter stickers made the page come together quickly and easily.

Country Charm
Becky Fleck, Columbus, Montana

SUPPLIES:

Patterned paper (Bo-Bunny Press, Chatterbox, Melissa Frances); letter stickers (Scenic Route Paper Co.); tag (Pressed Petals); button (Junkitz); fabric (Shoebox Trims); chipboard flower (Bazzill); frame (My Mind's Eye)

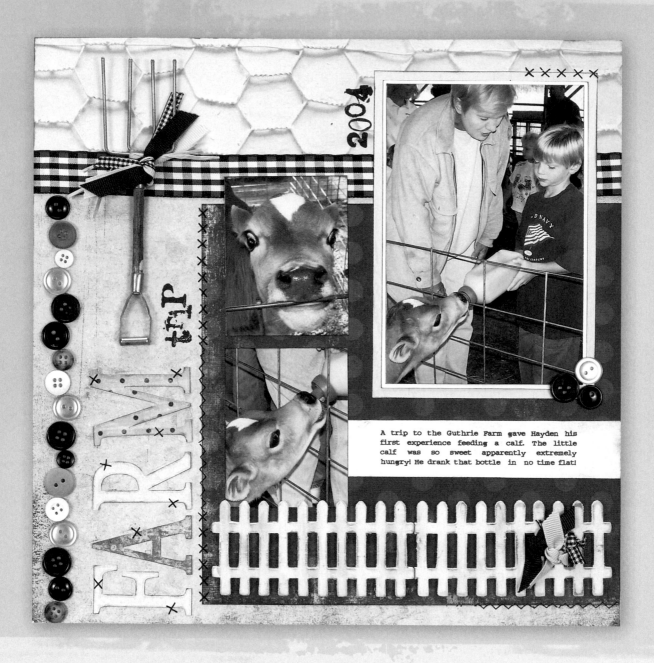

A trip to the Guthrie Farm gave Hayden his first experience feeding a calf. The little calf was so sweet apparently extremely hungry! He drank that bottle in no time flat!

KATHY'S LAYOUT truly makes you feel as if you're down on the farm with her. The simple background color blocking and rub-on stitch accents brought her design together in a snap. The charming white picket fence and pitch-fork—along with the gingham ribbon—lend a traditional country feel to the page. Letter stickers and a button border complete the farmstead look.

Farm Trip
Kathy Fesmire, Athens, Tennessee

SUPPLIES:

Patterned paper (Daisy D's, My Mind's Eye); ribbon (Offray); rub-ons (Dee's Designs, Doodlebug Design); fence, pitchfork (Crafts, Etc.); letter stickers (My Mind's Eye); blue crackle (Provo Craft); stamping ink; buttons; cardstock

A PHOTO OF BABY BRINLEY happily tucked into Mommy's sweater is perfect for this layout exuding all the warmth and affection felt by its subjects. Amy chose weathered papers that had patterns reflecting a folk art/Americana theme. She inked and dry-brushed the papers and accents to carry through the distressed feel. Lastly, she added chicken wire and gingham ribbon for a true touch of the country.

Warm Whispers
Amy Farnsworth, Brighton, Colorado

SUPPLIES:

Patterned paper (Autumn Leaves, FoofaLa, Rusty Pickle); wooden frame (Chatterbox); chipboard letters (Heidi Swapp); tag, wings (Autumn Leaves, FoofaLa); rub-ons (FontWerks); ribbon (May Arts); letter stickers (American Crafts); stamping ink; chicken wire; fabric; cardstock

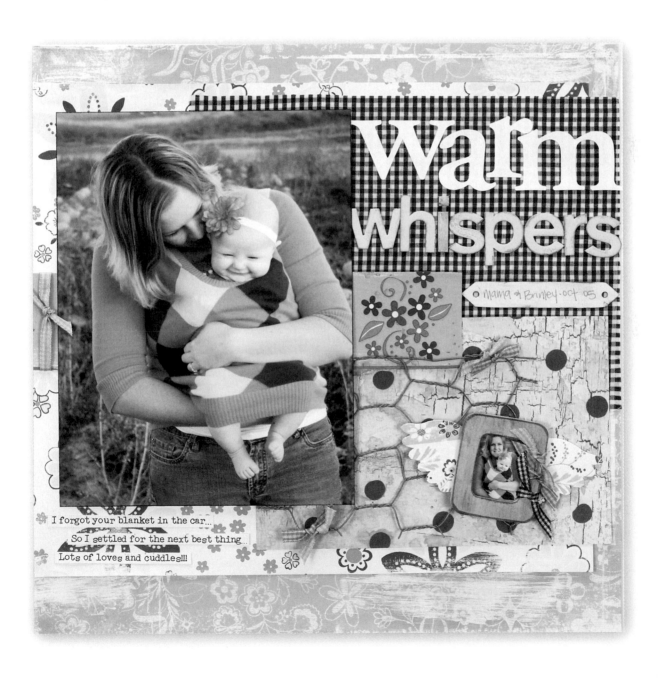

A TODDLER'S SWEET SMILE complements this French country layout. Amber started by layering her distressed background paper comprised of darker colors to lend a more masculine feel. She completed the background by sewing the edges with a simple straight stitch on her sewing machine. She painted wooden frames to match the paper and sanded the edges. The journaling block was printed on an adhesive-backed transparency and placed over her tag, tied with red twill.

10
Amber Baley, Waupun, Wisconsin

SUPPLIES:

Patterned paper (Daisy D's); wooden frames and tag (Chatterbox); chipboard hearts (Heidi Swapp); transparency (Grafix); stamping ink; acrylic paint

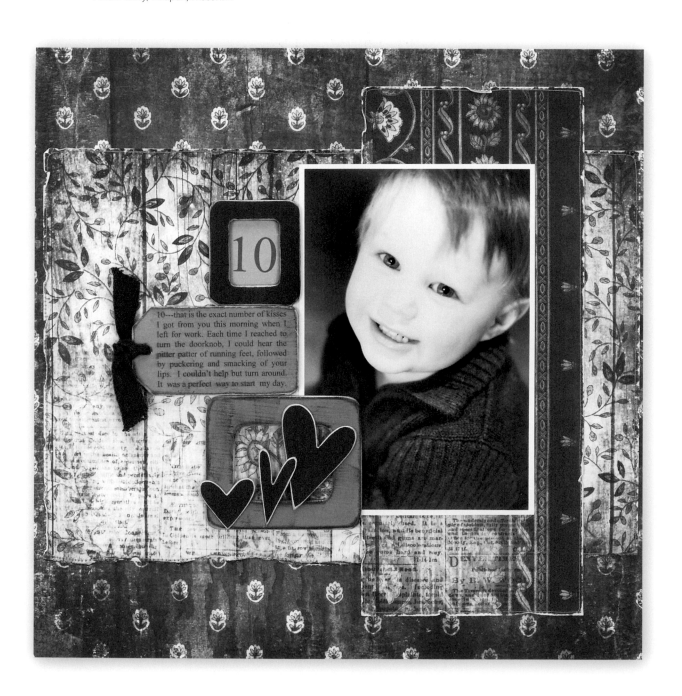

10---that is the exact number of kisses I got from you this morning when I left for work. Each time I reached to turn the doorknob, I could hear the pitter patter of running feet, followed by puckering and smacking of your lips. I couldn't help but turn around. It was a perfect way to start my day.

My Paris layout with journaling:

When I was in college I often dreamt of going to Paris. As I learned more about the city I fell in love with the language, the culture and the sights. Well, years have gone by and it seems like an actual trip there was just not meant to be.

However, while in Las Vegas this past February I dined at "The Paris" hotel. When I stepped into the building I was instantly reminded of my long-lost dream. Everything was exactly as I had thought it would be! My little dining room was a perfect rendition of a French village complete with flowering window boxes.

I fell in love with the fabulous food, the dainty pastries and the quaint décor. Realizing that this may be the closest that I ever get to Europe I now claim this experience as my own little Paris!

FOR SHARON, PARADISE IS IN PARIS—whether it be the real city in France or the famous hotel in Las Vegas! She chose two patterns of paper that fit her Parisian theme, and from these she cut wide strips to use for journaling and fill-in areas. Around the photo, she hand-trimmed squares to create a fitted "stone" look. The ribbon, lace and paper daisies positioned below the photo mimic a terra-cotta window box of fresh flowers. Lastly, she crackled her title letters to give them a weathered appearance.

My Paris
Sharon Laakkonen, Superior, Wisconsin

SUPPLIES:

Patterned paper (Daisy D's, Imagination Project); chipboard letters (Heidi Swapp); paper flowers (Prima); lace, ribbon (Michaels); mini brads (Queen & Co.); distress ink; crackle medium; acrylic paint; staples; white pen; cardstock

OUR tradition

TOP TEN LIST
1. Trip to pumpkin patch
2. Photos w/ pumpkins
3. Jumping booth
4. Critters in the barn
5. Petting zoo
6. Ride to fields to pick
7. Hay maze pumpkin
8. Little train ride
9. Time together
10. Do it again next year!

IN DESIGNING THIS FRENCH COUNTRY PAGE, Angelia wanted to spotlight a sepia-toned photo of her daughter during an annual trip to the pumpkin patch. She began by adding the red floral prints and stripes and accented them with the black prints. The splash of yellow, mini dots and gingham checks add to the playful but welcoming feel. Rub-ons and pre-printed letters made the title fast and easy to create. A preprinted journaling tag holds her handwritten top-ten list, while crocheted trim and black rickrack add texture and charm.

Our Tradition
Angelia Wigginton, Belmont, Mississippi

SUPPLIES:

Patterned paper (7 Gypsies, Daisy D's, K & Company); journaling tag (7 Gypsies); rub-on letters (Mustard Moon); letter stickers (FoofaLa); leather flower, button (Making Memories); rickrack (Doodlebug Design); rub-on swirl (Basic Grey); photo corners (Canson); silk flower, crocheted trim (source unknown); staples

TORN AND DISTRESSED PAPERS, frayed gingham fabric and inked edges add a folk art feel to this charming layout featuring a happy couple in love. Nic used large color blocking, a stamped title and dry-brushed paint to create the layout quickly and easily.

Two
Nic Howard, Pukekohe, New Zealand
Photo: Jacob Howard, Pukekohe, New Zealand

SUPPLIES:

Patterned paper (American Crafts); tag (Rusty Pickle); paper distresser (Heidi Swapp); decoupage medium; acrylic paint; stamps (PSX Design); solvent ink; gingham fabric (source unknown); cardstock; font (Two Peas in a Bucket)

TWO PEOPLE POSING
TWO CHILDREN TRYING
TO HELP TAKE PICTURES
MANY PERFECT MOMENTS.
LOTS OF CAMERA TIPS.
JUST ONE PHOTO IN FOCUS.
OF THE TWO OF US.

TWO

[petticoat] TO [prairie]

Stillwater County, Montana is littered with abandoned farms and homesteads, scored by old barns, shacks and cabins. Driving around to these once prosperous farms satisfies my fascination of an era long ago. As I peek into windows that no longer contain glass, I often find myself imagining the family that once occupied the home, barely able to envision the hardship and struggles of their everyday life.

One of my favorites is the Malone farm. Fillah A. Malone, a young widow with five small children, was one of only a handful of women to successfully homestead a Montana farm in 1917. With sheer grit, determination and courage, she raised her children alone on the desolate Montana prairie and continued to cultivate her land until her death in 1958.

BECKY'S INQUISITIVE NATURE led her to document one of the many abandoned homesteads on the Montana prairie. To keep in line with the weathered condition of the house and farm equipment, she converted her photos to sepia and chose "saddle leather" patterned papers with a distressed and worn feel. A computer-generated title combined with epoxy letter stickers made a quick and easy title. Frayed ribbon and button brads with an antique charm complete this intriguing heritage page.

Petticoat to Prairie
Becky Fleck, Columbus, Montana

SUPPLIES:

Patterned paper (K & Company, Paper Patch); typewriter keys, button brads (K & Company); fabric strips (Weavewerks); vellum (Bazzill); distress ink

SAMUEL CREATED THIS PAGE as a touching tribute to his mother, who will always be remembered by those who loved her. The most striking element is the combination of the large focal photo of Vaida in her younger years and a smaller circular photo to evoke the span of her rich lifetime. Samuel used papers and embellishments with a vintage quality to support the heritage theme. He paper-pieced and layered his elements, but kept everything basic and simple.

Vaida: Remember
Samuel Cole, Stillwater, Minnesota

SUPPLIES:

Patterned paper (Daisy D's, Design Originals, K & Company, Scenic Route Paper Co., Tapestry); letter stamps (Hero Arts); metal frame (K & Company); tag, border stickers (Me & My Big Ideas); ribbon, brads (Making Memories); hardware stickers (Sandylion); nameplate (7 Gypsies); stamp (PSX Design); ink

A love that is

TIMELESS

Today is our 12th anniversary. It's hard to believe that much time has gone so quickly. But then again it's getting harder to remember what life was like before you. And I know this is only the beginning. Feb 2006

ALTHOUGH THIS PHOTO of Kathleen and her husband is recent, it was printed in sepia to lend an antique feeling. Kathleen chose vintage-looking patterned paper and sanded the edges of the paper and the photo as a quick and easy yet effective technique. She applied antique-looking stickers, pre-made die-cut letters and frayed cotton lace as embellishments to enhance the vintage feel. Handwritten journaling lends further authenticity.

A Love That Is Timeless
Kathleen Summers, Roseville, California

SUPPLIES

Patterned paper (Crossed Paths); cotton lace (Making Memories); stickers (Crafty Secrets)

KI PAYS TRIBUTE to her much-loved companion of the four-legged variety on this heartwarming page. She used two quick and easy techniques—inking and sanding—to create a distressed, worn appearance on her patterned papers, chipboard letters, tag, lace and photos. She used buttons to decorate not only because they can be adhered in a flash, but because they lend a vintage feel. And she cut the patterned paper border on the left to give it a scalloped edge, which she associates with vintage linen.

A Sweet Soul
Ki Kruk, Sherwood Park, Alberta, Canada

SUPPLIES:

Patterned paper, brads (A2Z Essentials); photo turns, metal tab, tag, transparency (7 Gypsies); chipboard letters (We R Memory Keepers); lace, staples (Making Memories); distress ink; buttons (Bazzill); Typist font

The best way to describe Bear is that she is *A Sweet Soul*. Her eyes show a kindness and gentleness that makes her so easy to adore. At six years old, she is still as playful as when she was a pup. Walks are definitely her favorite activity that she repays with loyalty and unconditional love.

April 2006

PERFECT

POUT

Oh Brinley! why so sad? you have the cutest little pouty face! it's definitely a lot cuter than mine, that's for sure! chin up girlie! life can't be that bad. you have a family that adores you into itty bitty pieces! always remember that, okay! ♡, mommy

AMY DECIDED A CHIC BOHEMIAN LOOK was just the ticket for this page about her baby's pouty but precious facial expression. To add humor she posed alongside her baby girl and donned a "pout" herself. For her design, she sewed gathered fabric to the bottom of the page to add texture and dimension. The gold accents support the Bohemian theme while the large swirl grounds the page.

Perfect Pout
Amy Farnsworth, Brighton, Colorado

SUPPLIES:

Patterned paper (We R Memory Keepers); buttons, floss (Making Memories); chipboard letters (Li'l Davis Designs); letter stickers (FoofaLa); photo turn (7 Gypsies); flowers (Shason, Inc.); swirl frame (Everlasting Keepsakes); felt; fabric; pen; cardstock

THIS GIGGLY GIRL is front and center on Greta's page. She used deep colors as well as felt, scrolls and the metal medallion to convey a Bohemian feel. To make the page quickly and easily, she used very little paper and grouped all the elements around the photo. The colors of the paper and embellishments make for a rich layout that doesn't require a lot of extra details or work.

Laugh
Greta Hammond, Goshen, Indiana

SUPPLIES:

Patterned paper (Autumn Leaves, Daisy D's); medallion, buttons (Making Memories); chipboard letters (Heidi Swapp); rub-on scrolls (Dee's Designs); felt (Artgirlz); cardstock

Liam makes a funny face. You crack a smile.

Liam sings a silly song. You chuckle a little.

Liam dances a funny jig. You start to giggle.

Liam flops on the floor. You

LAUGH

out loud. And so our day goes.

THE BOHEMIAN STYLE originated in France, so Deb knew that her pictures from Paris would be perfect for this layout. However, rather than just making the page another record of "who, what, where and when," she chose the theme of reflection on how she would love to return to the city. She found the architecture so inspiring that she used bold colors and curves to mimic the feel of what she saw on her visit abroad. Comprised entirely of paper, photos and stickers, the artful page was easy to pull together.

Take Me Back to Paris
Deb Perry, Newport News, Virginia

SUPPLIES:

Patterned paper (7 Gypsies, K & Company, Paperwerx, Sassafras Lass); letter stickers (American Crafts, Sticker Studio); rub-on letters (Imagination Project, KI Memories); pen

THIS SILLY YET SOPHISTICATED little girl is celebrated in Lisa's endearing layout. Lisa used stickers and rub-ons for her title, which she intentionally mismatched to add visual interest. She tore the brown paper to add a textured edge, and she tied velvet ribbon to the top and middle to add some Bohemian flair and to balance the page. She finished by machine stitching a few edges with brown thread to match the ribbon.

Ragamuffin Princess
Lisa VanderVeen, Mendham, New Jersey

SUPPLIES:

Patterned paper (American Crafts); brads, ribbon (Making Memories); rub-ons (Basic Grey, Rusty Pickle); chipboard frame (Li'l Davis Designs); metal strip (Pressed Petals); stickers (EK Success); paper flowers (Prima); cardstock; Harrington font (Microsoft)

SHARON BEGAN BY CHOOSING a selection of rich colors and a variety of textured embellishments. To add a sense of movement to the page, she traced a simple wave pattern onto her patterned papers, cut them out and stitched them to the cardstock background. She saved space and time by printing her journaling over the photo. The glass beads, felt flowers, floral trim and unique font all add to the popular Bohemian look.

My Home
Sharon Laakkonen, Superior, Wisconsin

SUPPLIES:

Patterned paper (Basic Grey, Paper Crate); velvet ribbon (Rusty Pickle); buttons (FoofaLa); glass beads (Michaels); floral trim, staples (Making Memories); letter stickers (Basic Grey); diamond glaze (JudiKins); distress ink (Ranger); fabric; felt; thread; green ribbon; cardstock; digital brushes (Scrap Artist); Olive Oil font

Bohemian? Yes, that is my heritage. My grandparents moved to the United States from Czechoslavakia in the early 1900s. I have always loved learning about their culture...their homeland...their people. I even learned to speak their language when I was little. When I see Bohemian items now I am instantly attracted to them. I cannot help it. I know it is in my blood! I love the colors, the textures, the richness. Each item takes me a little bit closer to my home.

my Home

What I love about you

We are Family

EVERLASTING

ALWAYS, FOREVER

I love you...
unmistakably
undeniably,

I *Adore* you.
Everyday it grows
a little *deeper*,
a little *richer*,
a little *sweeter*.
It's all your ways;
it's all the little things
you do that put a

Smile

on my face and hold
that place in my
heart.
There are no words
that can truly
describe it; it is
simply a part of me;
the *very best part* of
me. For you, I am

Thankful.
For this love I am
forever grateful.
More than anything
else that I know...
I know that
I love you.

MELODEE EFFECTIVELY COMBINED a light-hearted photo with a darker color scheme to produce this engaging tribute to her son. She used a distressed vintage-looking paper and lace from a thrift shop to create an old, worn look. The rich browns and scripty font add style and verve. To boost the design's impact in a quick way, she layered a pre-printed transparency over the entire layout.

What I Love About You
Melodee Langworthy, Rockford, Michigan

SUPPLIES:

Patterned paper, black clip (7 Gypsies); rub-ons (Creative Imaginations, Scenic Route Paper Co.); index tab (Die Cuts With A View); stamping ink

THE SPECIAL MOMENTS between mother and daughter are worth documentation. Here, Trudy used a selection of papers and colors that reflect the Bohemian style to do so. The addition of lace, ribbon and satin trim creates the textures associated with this elegant style. Sewing proved to be a quick way to attach additional items to the page while adding design details at the same time. In place of a long journaling block, Trudy stamped short phrases to describe her soon-to-be teenage daughter.

Moments
Trudy Sigurdson, Victoria, British Columbia, Canada
Photo: Alex Sigurdson, Victoria, British Columbia, Canada

SUPPLIES:

Patterned paper, photo corners, profile tag (7 Gypsies); epoxy letters, bookplate (Li'l Davis Designs); flourish stamp (Heidi Swapp); charms (Nunn Designs); letter stamps (Provo Craft, PSX Design); date stamp (JustRite Stampers); walnut ink tags (Rusty Pickle); stamping ink; ribbon (My Mind's Eye); brads, cardstock

A LITTLE GIRL'S ADORATION for her grandmother couldn't be better illustrated than in Nic's touching piece. Nic decided to use deep colors to stay in line with the Bohemian style's gypsy, hippy vibe. Large fabric shapes create texture and depth over a large amount of the page, and patterned paper with lots of color and detail adds striking visual impact. Strips across the bottom of the page complete the detail.

Show Me, Nanny
Nic Howard, Pukekohe, New Zealand

SUPPLIES:

Patterned paper (Basic Grey); wooden letters, chipboard letters and flowers (Li'l Davis Designs); chipboard swirls (Fancy Pants Designs); decoupage medium; fabric (source unknown); solvent ink; mesh

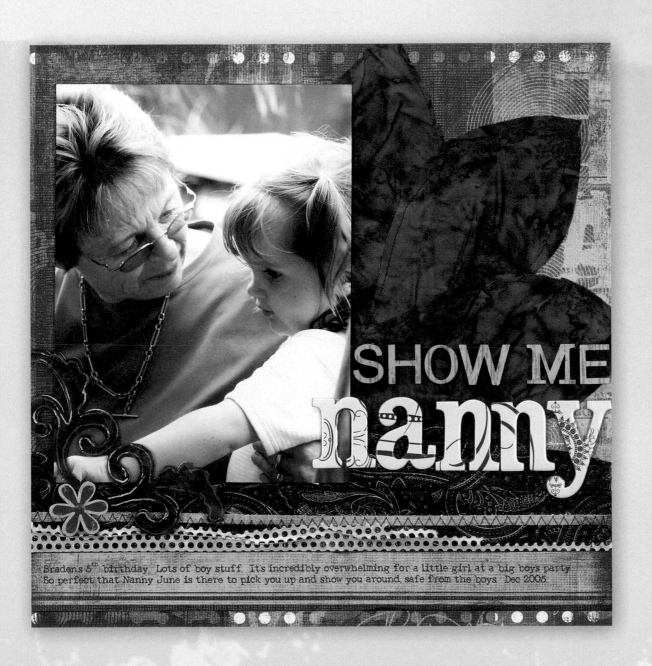

SHOW ME nanny

Bradens 5th birthday. Lots of boy stuff. It's incredibly overwhelming for a little girl at a big boys party. So perfect that Nanny June is there to pick you up and show you around, safe from the boys. Dec 2005.

When I first saw the Eiffel Tower I was amazed at just how huge it was! To stand underneath it and look up was such a spectacular sight! I took the elevator to the very top and looked out over the city. Though it wasn't until the sun went down that I really saw the *Magic of Paris!* February 2004

The magic *of* *Paris*

A NIGHTTIME SNAPSHOT of the famous French tower that rises above the city of lights illuminates Kim's page with a perfect golden glow. She used sandpaper and an edge distresser to quickly age the edges of the striking photos. To construct a quick photo corner, she cleverly folded over a piece of lace and secured it with a stick pin. She added chalk along her torn edges on the bottom of the page to quickly give the design an aged feeling. Her journaling tells of her enchantment with this magical city.

The Magic of Paris
Kim Moreno, Tucson, Arizona

SUPPLIES:

Patterned paper (Diane's Daughters); brads (Making Memories); stickpin (Nunn Design); flashcard (7 Gypsies); cardstock; Attic, Blackladder ITC fonts (Microsoft)

THIS "DAY IN THE LIFE" CHRONICLE celebrates the unique person her son is despite his typical, everyday kid's routine. To create this page, Holly simply layered rich and bold patterned papers. To add some dimension, she layered large diamonds in the background and continued the theme of diamonds as backing for the title. She used a simple strip journaling technique but added a fun twist by hanging the strips from the top. And she custom-made the transparency by scanning a watch face from a magazine ad, enlarging and cropping it in Photoshop, and printing it on the transparency.

Today You
Holly Corbett, Central, South Carolina

SUPPLIES:

Image-editing software (Adobe); patterned paper, rub-ons (Basic Grey); chipboard letter and parenthesis (Heidi Swapp); brads, stamping ink, acrylic paint (Making Memories); letter stamps (FontWerks); die-cut tag and letters (QuickKutz); photo corner punch (EK Success); transparency; cardstock

source guide

The following companies manufacture products featured in this book. Check your local retailers to find these materials, or go to a company's Web site for the latest products. Please note that we have made every attempt to properly credit the items mentioned in this book. We apologize to any company we have listed incorrectly, and we would appreciate hearing from you.

7 Gypsies
(877) 749-7797
www.sevengypsies.com

A2Z Essentials
(419) 663-2869
www.a2zessentials.com

Adobe Systems
Incorporated
(866) 766-2256
www.adobe.com

Advantus Corp.
(904) 482-0091
www.advantus.com

American Crafts
(801) 226-0747
www.americancrafts.com

American Tag Company
(800) 223-3956
www.americantag.net

American Traditional Designs®
(800) 448-6656
www.americantraditional.com

Anna Griffin, Inc.
(888) 817-8170
www.annagriffin.com

Artgirlz
www.artgirlz.com

Autumn Leaves
(800) 588-6707
www.autumnleaves.com

Basic Grey™
(801) 451-6006
www.basicgrey.com

Bazzill Basics Paper
(480) 558-8557
www.bazzillbasics.com

Beadery®, The
(401) 539-2432
www.thebeadery.com

Berwick Offray, LLC
(800) 344-5533
www.offray.com

Bo-Bunny Press
(801) 771-4010
www.bobunny.com

Canson®, Inc.
(800) 628-9283
www.canson-us.com

Chatterbox, Inc.
(208) 939-9133
www.chatterboxinc.com

Cherry Arte
(212) 465-3495
www.cherryarte.com

Collage Press
(435) 656-4611
www.collagepress.com

Crafts, Etc. Ltd.
(800) 888-0321
www.craftsetc.com

Crafty Secrets
Publications
(888) 597-8898
www.craftysecrets.com

Creative Imaginations
(800) 942-6487
www.cigift.com

Creative Memories®
(800) 468-9335
www.creativememories.com

Crossed Paths™
(972) 393-3755
www.crossedpaths.net

Dafont
www.dafont.com

Daisy D's Paper Company
(888) 601-8955
www.daisydspaper.com

Déjà Views
(800) 243-8419
www.dejaviews.com

Diane's Daughters®
(801) 621-8392
www.dianesdaughters.com

Die Cuts With A View
(801) 224-6766
www.diecutswithaview.com

DMC Corp.
(973) 589-0606
www.dmc.com

Doodlebug Design™ Inc.
(801) 966-9952
www.doodlebug.ws

Educational Insights
(800) 995-4436
www.edin.com

EK Success™, Ltd.
(800) 524-1349
www.eksuccess.com

Everlasting Keepsakes
(816) 896-7037
www.everlastingkeepsakes.com

Fancy Pants Designs, LLC
(801) 779-3212
www.fancypantsdesigns.com

Fiskars®, Inc.
(800) 950-0203
www.fiskars.com

FontWerks
(604) 942-3105
www.fontwerks.com

FoofaLa
(402) 330-3208
www.foofala.com

Frost Creek Charms
(763) 684-0074
www.frostcreekcharms.com

Grafix®
(800) 447-2349
www.grafix.com

Happy Hammer, The
(303) 690-3883
www.thehappyhammer.com

Heidi Grace Designs, Inc.
(608) 294-4509
www.heidigrace.com

Heidi Swapp/Advantus
Corporation
(904) 482-0092
www.heidiswapp.com

Hero Arts® Rubber Stamps, Inc.
(800) 822-4376
www.heroarts.com

Hobby Lobby Stores, Inc.
www.hobbylobby.com

Hot Off the Press
(800) 227-9595
www.b2b.hotp.com

Imagination Project, Inc.
(513) 860-2711
www.imaginationproject.com

Inkadinkado® Rubber Stamps
(800) 888-4652
www.inkadinkado.com

Jen Harrison
www.mrs.rismo.com

Jo-Ann Stores
(888) 739-4120
www.joann.com

Junkitz™
(732) 792-1108
www.junkitz.com

JustRite® Stampers / Millenium
Marking Company
(847) 806-1750
www.justritestampers.com

K & Company
(888) 244-2083
www.kandcompany.com

Karen Foster Design
(801) 451-9779
www.karenfosterdesign.com

KI Memories
(972) 243-5595
www.kimemories.com

Lä Dé Dä
(225) 755-8899
www.ladeda.com

Li'l Davis Designs
(949) 838-0344
www.lildavisdesigns.com

Limited Edition
Rubberstamps
(650) 594-4242
www.limitededitionrs.com

Magic Scraps™
(972) 238-1838
www.magicscraps.com

MaisyMo™ Designs
(973) 907-7262
www.maisymo.com

Making Memories
(800) 286-5263
www.makingmemories.com

Mara-Mi, Inc.
(800) 627-2648
www.mara-mi.com

May Arts
(800) 442-3950
www.mayarts.com

me & my BIG ideas®
(949) 883-2065
www.meandmybigideas.com

Melissa Frances/Heart & Home,
Inc.
(905) 686-9031
www.melissafrances.com

Memory Creators
(714) 848-0510
www.memorycreators.com

MJ Zoom
(877) 465-9666
www.mjzoom.com

MOD - my own design
(303) 641-8680
www.mod-myowndesign.com

Mrs. Grossman's Paper Company
(800) 429-4549
www.mrsgrossmans.com

Mustard Moon™
(408) 299-8542
www.mustardmoon.com

My Mind's Eye™, Inc.
(800) 665-5116
www.mymindseye.com

Nunn Design
(360) 379-3557
www.nunndesign.com

Offray - see Berwick Offray, LLC

Paper Company, The / ANW
Crestwood
(800) 525-3196
www.anwcrestwood.com

Paper Patch®, The
(800) 397-2737
www.paperpatch.com

Paperwerks
(866) 479-0868
www.paperwerks.com

Plaid Enterprises, Inc.
(800) 842-4197
www.plaidonline.com

Pressed Petals
(800) 748-4656
www.pressedpetals.com

Prima Marketing, Inc.
(909) 627-5532
www.primamarketinginc.com

Provo Craft®
(888) 577-3545
www.provocraft.com

Prym-Dritz Corporation
www.dritz.com

PSX Design™
(800) 782-6748
www.psxdesign.com

Queen & Co.
(858) 485-5132
www.queenandcompany.com

QuicKutz, Inc.
(801) 765-1144
www.quickutz.com

Ranger Industries, Inc.
(800) 244-2211
www.rangerink.com

Reminisce Papers
(319) 358-9777
www.shopreminisce.com

Rusty Pickle
(801) 746-1045
www.rustypickle.com

Sandylion Sticker Designs
(800) 387-4215
www.sandylion.com

Sassafras Lass
(801) 269-1331
www.sassafraslass.com

Scenic Route Paper Co.
(801) 785-0761
www.scenicroutepaper.com

Scrapsupply
(615) 777-3953
www.scrapsupply.com

Scraptivity
(800) 393-2151
www.scraptivity.com

Scrapvillage
www.scrapvillage.com

Scrapworks, LLC
(801) 363-1010
www.scrapworks.com

SEI, Inc.
(800) 333-3279
www.shopsei.com

Shabby Princess
www.shabbyprincess.com

Shason, Inc. / Silk Trading
Company
(804) 643-6466
www.silktradingco.com

Shoebox Trims
(303) 697-5942
www.shoeboxtrims.com

Sizzix®
(866) 742-4447
www.sizzix.com

Sticker Studio
(208) 322-2465
www.stickerstudio.com

Strano Designs
(508) 454-4615
www.stranodesigns.com

Technique Tuesday, LLC
(503) 644-0473
www.techniquetuesday.com

Therm O Web
(800) 323-0799
www.thermoweb.com
Sampled on pages: 41, 52,
73, 101

Tsukineko®, Inc.
(800) 769-6633
wwwtsukineko.com

Two Peas in a Bucket
(888) 896-7327
www.twopeasinabucket.com

Urban Lily
www.urbanlily.com

Wal-Mart Stores, Inc.
(800) WALMART
www.walmart.com

We R Memory Keepers
(801) 539-5000
www.weronthenet.com

Weavewerks
www.weavewerks.com

Westrim® Crafts
(800) 727-2727
www.westrimcrafts.com

Wildflower Stamps
www.wildflowerstamps.com

Wrights® Ribbon Accents
(877) 597-4448
www.wrights.com

additional credits & supplies

Page 12
GRAPHIC
Linda created a linear page by cutting a curved shape in the blue cardstock to add interest and movement. She used one enlarged photo as the focal point. By sticking to three main colors and white, the layout remains clean and uncluttered. Using patterned paper, pre-cut chipboard letters and fun rub-ons all help to add interest to the page and keep it quick and easy.

Glee
Linda Harrison, Sarasota, Florida

Supplies: Patterned paper, chipboard letters (Scenic Route Paper Co.); photo anchors (Queen & Co.); brads (Junkitz); cardstock; SP Sara Jean font (Scrapsupply)

Page 36
SASSY
Nic used coordinating papers with large floral prints to achieve this sassy look. She trimmed the flowers from one sheet of patterned paper to use them as accents. The bright pink, orange, green and blue add vibrance and energy. A touch of black ink on the edges of the patterned papers ties everything together in a cohesive manner.

Dude
Nic Howard, Pukekohe, New Zealand
Photo: Jessie Baldwin, Las Vegas, Nevada

Supplies: Patterned paper (FancyPants Designs); letter stickers (Basic Grey); stamping ink; cardstock; In A Hurry font (Two Peas in a Bucket)

Page 58
URBAN
This page has as much grit and determination as Jill's athletic son featured in the action photo. Jill enlarged her focal photo, then trimmed her circles, layered the paper and placed the transparency on top. She placed letter stickers over the transparency. To add black color to the chipboard letters, she used a basic black pen. She then added standard staples to adhere the title to the bottom of the layout.

Got Game?
Jill Jackson-Mills, Roswell, Georgia

Supplies: Patterned paper (Paper House Productions, Scenic Route Paper Co.); diamond plate embossed paper; rub-on border (EK Success); chipboard letters (Making Memories, Pressed Petals); metal words (Making Memories); transparency (Creative Imaginations); acrylic word (Li'l Davis Designs); letter stickers (Basic Grey)

Page 68
FUN AND FUNKY
Heather captured the spirit of a fun picture in this funky layout. She used bright colors and created a free-form shape to frame her picture that serves double duty to hold her journaling. She hand-drew her title in a fun way to add to the freestyle look.

Quirky Girl
Heather Preckel, Swannanoa, North Carolina

Supplies: Patterned paper, stickers (Sandylion); buttons (Junkitz); ribbon (Morex Corp.); adhesive; pen; cardstock

Page 88
ROMANTIC
To achieve the trés chic look in a quick and easy way, Diana chose products that already had a distressed look. She used rub-ons and stickers for the title and journaling, then used an edge distresser on the edges of the papers to add a little bit of texture. The black-and-white photo exudes true beauty.

Beautiful
Diana Hudson, Bakersfield, California

Supplies: Patterned paper (K & Company); lace and velvet trim, rub-on title, letter stickers, jewelry tag, gems, corsage pin (Making Memories); rub-on date, buttons (Autumn Leaves); border sticker (My Mind's Eye); paper flowers (Prima); decorative tape (Heidi Swapp); vintage buttons; staples

index

Additional Credits & Instructions, 126

Bohemian, 114-123

Close-up photos, 22, 27, 40, 42, 52-53, 66, 98, 115, 117, 122-123
Contributing Artists, 3

Distressed, 109-113
Doodles, 71-72, 75

Fashion-inspired, 40-45
French country, 98-108
Fun & Funky overview, 10
Fun & Funky trademarks, 70

Geometric shapes, 18-19, 73-74, 82
Graphic overview, 7
Graphic trademarks, 14

Heritage photos, 101, 110-111

Large photos, 16, 18, 24, 28, 30, 33, 64, 77, 83, 111

Media-inspired, 30-34, 61, 82-87
Monograms, 47

Photo effects, 84, 86
Photomontage/photo series, 17, 23, 25, 29, 34, 45, 72, 102-103, 116

Retro pages, 76-81
Rhythm, 20
Romantic overview, 11
Romantic trademarks, 90
Rule of thirds, 23

Sassy overview, 8
Sassy trademarks, 38
Shiny accents, 52-57
Source Guide, 124-125

Table of contents, 4
Trés chic, 91-97
Type, 24-29, 87

Urban overview, 9
Urban trademarks, 60

What's Your Style?, 6
White space, 15

Learn more with these fine titles from Memory Makers Books!

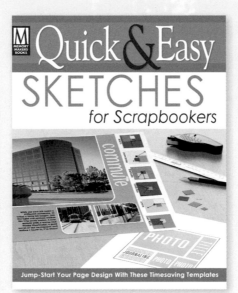

200 all new timesaving layouts you can create in one hour or less

Simply Graphic
If you love scrapbook pages with clean lines, bold fonts, impactful photos and lots of open space, you'll love the 176 layouts featured in this book. Learn how concept, type, image and layout contribute to this popular style.

ISBN-13: 978-1-892127-78-5
ISBN-10: 1-892127-78-4
paperback • 128 pgs. • #Z0018

Quick & Easy Sketches for Scrapbookers
Take the guesswork out of page design with these user-friendly sketches adaptable to any page theme. Over 260 page-design possibilities.

ISBN-13: 978-1-892127-64-4
ISBN-10: 1-892127-64-8
paperback • 96 pgs. • #33436

More Quick & Easy Scrapbook Pages
Learn to make cool pages fast with these never-before-seen timesaving layouts. Over 200 scrapbook pages featuring today's cutting-edge styles and techniques.

ISBN-13: 978-1-892127-56-3
ISBN-10: 1-892127-56-3
paperback • 128 pgs. • #33360

These and other Memory Makers Books are available from your local art or craft retailer, bookstore or online supplier.